PROMOTING PUPPETS

The High Cost of Corporate Favoritisms

RAKESH SINGH

The Ghost in the Cubicle"

"Every office has a ghost. They were the one who stayed late, solved the problems no one else could touch, and possessed a quiet brilliance that kept the department afloat. But today, their desk is empty. They didn't leave for a better salary; they left because they realized that in this office, **competence is a currency that no longer buys growth.** > While the 'Ghost' was busy working, the 'Player' was busy lunching with the VP. While the 'Ghost' was fixing a system error, the 'Player' was claiming credit for the uptime. This book is the autopsy of the modern workplace—a look at how we've traded real talent for 'loyal' mediocrity, and why the people you need most are the ones you're driving out the door

Table of Contents

FROM THE AUTHOR

I didn't write this book as a rebel.
I wrote it as a witness.

After years inside corporate environments, I saw something deeply troubling—talent being ignored, honesty being punished, and favoritism being celebrated as leadership.

I saw good people slowly lose confidence.
I saw high performers grow quiet.
I saw offices full of noise but empty of courage.

And I realized something important:

Millions of professionals are suffering silently—not because they lack skills, but because they refuse to become puppets.

This book is not against organizations.
It is against unhealthy systems.

It is written for professionals who want to grow **without flattery**, succeed **without manipulation**, and protect their peace **without quitting their values**.

If this book helps you feel seen, grounded, and strong again—
then it has already done its job.

— **Rakesh Singh**
Author of *Under the Table*,AI Vs Human & *Man After Marriage*

.

Chapter 1: The Corporate Reality No One Warned Us About

Most of us enter corporate life with clean hearts and honest expectations.

We believe that if we work hard, stay sincere, respect deadlines, and deliver results, we will grow. We believe effort will be noticed, talent will be rewarded, and integrity will protect us. We believe offices are professional spaces where fairness exists, where intelligence matters, and where truth has value.

No one tells us that this belief will slowly break.

Not suddenly.
Not dramatically.
But quietly—day by day.

At first, everything feels right. The first job offer feels like validation. The ID card feels like identity. The office building feels like a promise. We tell our families proudly where we work. We imagine a future shaped by growth, learning, and recognition. We promise ourselves we will give our best.

And we do.

We stay late.
We skip lunches.
We take work home.
We solve problems that were never ours.
We protect the team's reputation even when no one is watching.

We believe this is how careers are built.

But slowly, cracks appear.

You notice that meetings are not about ideas anymore—they are about alignment. You notice that the loudest voice is not always the smartest one. You notice that the person who talks the most about loyalty gets praised more than the person who delivers results. You notice appreciation being selective, not sincere.

At first, you doubt yourself.

"Maybe I'm overthinking."
"Maybe this is just one incident."
"Maybe things will improve."

They rarely do.

That is when the real corporate reality introduces itself—the one no one warned us about.

Talent Is Visible — But Power Decides

Talent is never invisible. Good work is always seen. Excellence leaves fingerprints everywhere. Systems run better because of certain people. Teams survive pressure because of certain individuals. Deadlines are met because someone silently carries the weight.

Everyone knows who those people are.

But knowing is not the same as rewarding.

In corporate life, talent alone does not decide growth. Power does.

Power decides whose mistakes are forgiven.
Power decides whose success is celebrated.
Power decides whose name reaches leadership and whose effort stays buried in spreadsheets.

You start noticing that promotions don't always go to the most capable person. They go to the most connected one. The most compliant one. The one closest to power. The one who understands the politics better than the problem.

And that realization hurts.

Because you did everything right—but right was not enough.

You weren't lacking skill.
You weren't lacking commitment.
You were lacking proximity to power.

That is when disillusionment begins.

Performance Is Recorded — But Loyalty Is Rewarded

Corporate systems love data. Everything is tracked. KPIs, dashboards, performance reviews, metrics—nothing escapes documentation.

Your performance is recorded meticulously.

But when decisions are made, something else speaks louder than numbers: loyalty.

Not loyalty to work.
Not loyalty to values.
But loyalty to people.

You see average performers moving ahead because they are "trusted." You see mistakes ignored because the person is "close to the boss." You see excuses accepted because the relationship is strong.

Meanwhile, performers are told to "be patient."

Patience becomes the most dangerous word in corporate life. It is often used to delay justice, not deliver it.

And slowly, you learn an uncomfortable truth: performance keeps you employed, but loyalty decides how far you go.

This realization doesn't just affect careers—it affects confidence. You begin questioning your worth. You wonder if honesty was a mistake. You ask yourself whether being real has a cost you were never prepared to pay.

And that internal conflict is exhausting.

Truth Exists — But Flattery Travels Faster

Truth still exists in corporate spaces. People know what's wrong. They know what's inefficient. They know which decisions are flawed. They know when leadership is mistaken.

But truth moves slowly. Flattery moves fast.

Flattery is easier to digest. It doesn't challenge egos. It doesn't threaten authority. It doesn't demand accountability. It makes people feel powerful, respected, admired—even when they are wrong.

So flattery becomes currency.

People learn how to speak carefully, not honestly. They learn how to agree publicly and criticize privately. They learn how to package lies politely. They learn how to tell the boss what they want to hear, not what they need to know.

Truth-tellers slowly become dangerous.
Not because they are wrong—but because they are real.

And reality is uncomfortable.

So truth is sidelined.
Flattery is promoted.
Silence is rewarded.

This is how environments become toxic—not through cruelty, but through dishonesty dressed as professionalism.

The Emotional Cost No One Talks About

What hurts most is not the politics itself.

It is the emotional confusion.

You start doubting your instincts. You hesitate before speaking. You measure words instead of expressing ideas.

You feel anxious before meetings. You carry work stress home—not because of workload, but because of unfairness.

You lie awake at night replaying conversations. You wonder if you should have spoken differently, praised more, stayed silent longer. You feel tired even when work is done.

And the most painful part?

You still care.

You care about quality.
You care about impact.
You care about doing the right thing.

But the system doesn't always care back.

That is when many people emotionally withdraw. They stop giving ideas. They stop going the extra mile. They do what is required—nothing more, nothing less. Not because they are lazy, but because hope has been bruised too many times.

This is the silent erosion of talent.

Understanding the Reality Without Losing Yourself

This chapter is not meant to make you bitter.

It is meant to make you aware.

Corporate reality is not black and white. Not all leaders are unfair. Not all systems are broken. But pretending politics doesn't exist is dangerous. It leaves good people unprepared and emotionally wounded.

Awareness is not cynicism.
Understanding is not surrender.

Once you see the reality clearly, you can protect yourself. You can choose responses instead of reactions. You can build skills that create independence. You can decide where to invest energy and where to detach.

Most importantly, you stop blaming yourself for a system that was never designed to be fair by default.

This book is not asking you to become a puppet.
It is asking you to stop being naive.

There is dignity in excellence.
There is strength in calm awareness.
There is power in choosing integrity—even when it costs more.

You are not weak for believing in merit.
You are brave.

The chapters ahead will not just expose the system—they will show you how to survive it without losing your peace, your self-respect, or your humanity.

Because the truth is simple:

Talent is visible—but power decides.
Performance is recorded—but loyalty is rewarded.
Truth exists—but flattery travels faster.

Knowing this doesn't make you smaller.
It makes you prepared.

Chapter 2: Promoting Puppets — How Favouritism Really Works

Favouritism rarely announces itself.
It doesn't come with a memo or a policy update.
It slips in quietly, wearing the mask of trust, loyalty, and "fit."

At first, you don't want to believe it exists. You tell yourself that promotions are earned, that appreciation is fair, that leaders see everything clearly. You assume there must be reasons you don't know yet. You give the system the benefit of doubt—because believing in fairness feels safer than questioning it.

But over time, patterns begin to repeat.

The same names keep rising.
The same voices keep getting heard.
The same mistakes keep getting ignored.

And slowly, painfully, you understand how favouritism really works.

When Praising the Boss Beats Solving Problems

In a healthy workplace, problems are welcomed because they lead to improvement. In a political workplace, problems are inconvenient—especially when they come from people who are not favourites.

You begin to notice something strange. The person who identifies risks is labeled "negative." The one who raises concerns is called "difficult." But the one who praises the boss endlessly—without contributing much—becomes "positive," "aligned," and "leadership material."

Meetings become performances.
Not of ideas—but of agreement.

People learn quickly what is rewarded. They stop asking hard questions. They stop challenging weak decisions. Instead, they nod. They agree. They echo. They compliment.

"Great thought, sir."
"Exactly what I was thinking."
"You always have the best clarity."

Meanwhile, real problems stay unresolved. Teams struggle silently. Systems weaken slowly. But the boss feels validated—and validation becomes more important than solutions.

This is when you realize a hard truth: in some offices, praising the boss beats solving problems.

And it hurts—not because appreciation exists, but because honesty disappears.

Gossip Becomes a Promotion Tool

Gossip is one of the most underestimated forces in corporate life.

It doesn't look powerful.
It doesn't appear on resumes.
It isn't mentioned in performance reviews.

Yet it quietly shapes perceptions.

Favourites often become information carriers. They know who said what. Who disagreed. Who looked unhappy in a meeting. Who questioned authority. They package gossip carefully—never as malice, but as "concern."

"I'm just telling you because I care."
"I thought you should know what people are saying."
"I didn't agree with them, but I wanted to inform you."

And just like that, reputations are shaped without evidence.

The person being gossiped about rarely gets a chance to explain. The narrative is already written. The damage is already done. Meanwhile, the messenger gains trust—not because they add value, but because they feed insecurity.

Over time, gossip becomes currency.
Not facts.
Not performance.
But whispers.

And when gossip starts influencing promotions, something deeply unfair happens: character assassination replaces evaluation.

Incompetence Survives Through Obedience

One of the most painful things to witness is incompetence surviving—not by improving, but by obeying.

Puppets don't ask questions.
They don't push back.
They don't threaten authority.

They follow instructions blindly, even when instructions are flawed. They don't care about outcomes as much as they care about approval. They protect the boss's image, even at the cost of team success.

And insecure leaders feel safe with them.

Because puppets don't outshine.
They don't expose weaknesses.
They don't bring uncomfortable truths.

They repeat.
They reflect.
They reinforce.

And so, incompetence survives—not because it performs, but because it obeys.

This doesn't mean favourites are always untalented. Some may have skills. But the system doesn't reward skill—it rewards submission. And that distinction matters deeply.

Because when obedience becomes the main qualification, excellence becomes a threat.

The Silent Damage to Real Talent

For talented, sincere professionals, this environment is emotionally draining.

You begin to question yourself.
You wonder if you're "too honest."
You feel punished for being straightforward.

You see your ideas used—but your name missing. You see your work praised—but credited elsewhere. You see growth happening around you—but never reaching you.

And worst of all, you start doubting your worth—not because you lack ability, but because you lack political alignment.

Many people don't quit immediately. They stay. They hope. They adjust. But something inside them slowly shuts down. The excitement fades. The hunger dulls. The joy disappears.

This is how talent doesn't just leave organizations—it leaves quietly, emotionally, long before resignation letters are written.

Reality Check: Puppets Don't Lead. They Repeat

Leadership requires courage.
Puppets require permission.

True leaders take responsibility. Puppets take instructions. Leaders protect teams. Puppets protect power.

Puppets don't build vision—they borrow it.
They don't create culture—they imitate it.
They don't solve problems—they hide them.

And while this may work short-term, it damages organizations long-term.

Because innovation doesn't come from obedience.
Growth doesn't come from fear.
Trust doesn't come from flattery.

Yet insecure leaders prefer echoes over excellence.

Why?

Because excellence asks questions.
Excellence exposes gaps.
Excellence demands growth.

And growth is uncomfortable for those who fear being surpassed.

Understanding Without Becoming Bitter

This chapter is not written to create anger. Anger burns energy that could be used to grow.

It is written to create clarity.

Once you understand how favouritism works, you stop internalizing rejection. You stop blaming yourself for someone else's insecurity. You stop seeking validation from a system that was never fair.

You learn to separate self-worth from workplace politics.

And most importantly, you begin preparing—not emotionally reacting.

Because puppets may get promoted, but they don't get fulfilled.
They don't earn respect—they borrow power.
And borrowed power always expires.

Your job is not to become louder than them.
Your job is to become stronger than the system.

That strength doesn't come from flattery.
It comes from self-respect, skill-building, emotional control, and timing.

The chapters ahead will show you how.

For now, remember this:

If you weren't chosen in a biased system, it doesn't mean you were unworthy.
It means you refused to become a puppet.

And that, quietly, is your greatest strength.

Absolutely. I'll extend the chapter seamlessly, keeping the same calm, heart-touching tone and deepening the contrast between **puppets and real talent**, without repeating ideas or breaking emotional flow.

The Temporary Safety of Puppets

Puppets often feel protected.
Not because they are strong—but because they are attached.

Their safety does not come from skill, credibility, or trust across the organization. It comes from proximity to power. As long as the boss remains in the same chair, their position feels secure. They walk with confidence borrowed from authority, not earned through competence.

But this safety is fragile.

It exists only under one condition: the boss must stay.

That is why puppets are always alert—not to improve, but to please. They watch moods more than metrics. They study reactions more than results. Their loyalty is not to the organization, the work, or the people—but to the individual who protects them.

And deep inside, even if they never say it aloud, they live with a quiet fear:

What if tomorrow the boss leaves?
What if leadership changes?
What if this umbrella disappears?

Why Puppets Are Always Insecure

Insecurity follows puppets like a shadow.

They may appear confident in meetings, but their confidence collapses the moment power shifts. They worry about new leaders. They fear new evaluations. They resist transparency because transparency exposes dependency.

They don't welcome change—they survive it cautiously.

That is why puppets often oppose new systems, new managers, or new ideas. Not because change is bad—but because change threatens their protection. A fair system would measure ability. A neutral leader would notice gaps. A performance-driven culture would ask uncomfortable questions.

And puppets are not prepared for that.

Their value is situational.
Their authority is conditional.
Their influence is temporary.

So they cling harder. Praise becomes louder. Gossip becomes sharper. Loyalty becomes exaggerated. Because without the boss, they know they must stand alone—and that terrifies them.

Real Talent Needs No Safety Umbrella

True talent operates differently.

Real talent doesn't look for protection—it creates value. It doesn't fear evaluation—it welcomes it. It doesn't depend on one leader's approval—it earns respect across teams, roles, and hierarchies.

When a boss changes, real talent adjusts.
When systems change, real talent learns.
When pressure increases, real talent performs.

Because their strength is internal, not positional.

They don't need to ask, *Who will save me?*
They ask, *What problem can I solve next?*

That is why real talent never feels threatened by leadership transitions. New bosses don't scare them—new opportunities excite them. They know that skill travels. Integrity travels. Reputation travels.

And no matter where they go, those qualities speak before they do.

The Freedom of Being Replaceable vs the Fear of Being Exposed

Ironically, puppets fear replacement more than anyone—despite appearing close to power.

Why?

Because deep down, they know they are not irreplaceable. They are interchangeable. Any other obedient voice could take their place if needed. Their role is not defined by excellence, but by availability.

Real talent, on the other hand, accepts replaceability without fear. They know no one is permanent—but they also know their capability will always create demand. This acceptance brings peace, not panic.

Puppets guard their position.
Talent builds its position.

Puppets hide behind people.
Talent stands on skills.

Puppets ask, *Am I still liked?*
Talent asks, *Am I still growing?*

Why Organizations Eventually Pay the Price

Organizations that promote puppets may feel stable in the short term. Decisions go unquestioned. Authority feels respected. Conflict appears minimal.

But underneath, cracks form.

Innovation slows.
Honest feedback disappears.
High performers disengage.

When leadership eventually changes—as it always does—the damage becomes visible. Puppets struggle to perform independently. Teams lose direction. Trust erodes. The organization pays the price for years of comfort-driven choices.

And by then, much of the real talent has already left—not in anger, but in silence.

A Quiet Truth for Those Who Feel Overlooked

If you are not favoured today, it may be because you don't fit into a system built on dependency.

And that is not a weakness.

It means you are capable of surviving without protection.
It means your confidence does not come from proximity to power.
It means you are not afraid of tomorrow's leadership.

You don't need someone to stay for you to succeed.
You don't need permission to grow.
You don't need a safety umbrella to stand tall.

Because real talent is weather-proof.

Puppets may look safe—but only while the storm is held back by one person.
Real talent walks into storms and builds shelter from skill, self-belief, and resilience.

And in the long run, that is the only kind of safety that lasts.

Chapter 3: When Performance Loses to Politics

At the beginning, most of us believe effort will speak for itself.

We arrive early.
We stay late.
We fix problems that are not even ours.
We take ownership, responsibility, and pride in our work.

And for a while, we wait.

We wait for recognition.
We wait for growth.
We wait for someone to notice.

But slowly, a strange pattern appears.

Hard work meets silence.
Politics meets applause.

The Day Merit Stops Making Noise

Performance is quiet. It does not shout. It does not advertise itself. It simply shows up—day after day—through results, reliability, and responsibility.

Politics, on the other hand, is loud.

It announces loyalty.
It exaggerates effort.
It performs visibility.

In many organizations, this difference decides careers.

You may complete a project flawlessly, but no one claps because no one saw you doing it. Meanwhile, someone else attends meetings, nods at the right moments, praises leadership, and suddenly their "contribution" becomes visible—even when their output is minimal.

This is when the realization hurts:

Doing the work is not the same as being seen doing the work.

And being seen matters more.

Performance vs Politics

Performance builds value.
Politics builds perception.

Performance improves systems.
Politics protects positions.

Performance asks, *How can we do better?*
Politics asks, *How can I look better?*

When organizations begin rewarding perception over value, the rules change silently. Not officially—but practically.

Suddenly:

- Results are optional
- Visibility is mandatory
- Integrity is inconvenient
- Silence becomes expensive

Those who focus on work start feeling invisible. Those who focus on politics start feeling powerful.

And this is where imbalance begins.

Promoted by Politics, Not Performance

One of the most painful moments in corporate life is watching someone grow—not because they performed better—but because they performed loyalty better.

You replay moments in your mind:

- *I delivered more.*

- *I handled tougher challenges.*
- *I stayed when others left.*

Yet promotions go elsewhere.

Not upward—but sideways into politics.

The promoted employee knows how to:

- Agree quickly
- Deflect blame
- Echo leadership opinions
- Control narratives

Their growth is not based on impact, but alignment.

And this creates a dangerous lesson for everyone watching:
Effort is optional. Strategy is everything.

Incompetence Wins—Quietly, Consistently

Incompetence rarely announces itself. It survives quietly under protection.

It hides behind meetings.
It hides behind hierarchy.
It hides behind influence.

Protected incompetence is one of the most damaging forces in any organization. Not because it exists—but because it is rewarded.

When incompetent individuals are promoted:

- Teams lose direction

- Strong performers lose motivation
- Decision quality declines
- Trust disappears

Yet the system continues—because politics is efficient. It is less demanding than excellence. It does not challenge leadership. It does not ask uncomfortable questions.

Incompetence feels safe.

And safety, in insecure environments, is valued more than capability.

The Emotional Cost of Being Overlooked

The biggest damage of politics is not professional—it is emotional.

You start doubting yourself.

Am I not good enough?
Am I missing something?
Should I become someone else to survive here?

This doubt is not born from failure—but from unfairness.

You feel tired, not because of work, but because effort feels meaningless. You stop sharing ideas. You stop volunteering. You do what is required—and nothing more.

Not out of laziness—but self-preservation.

Because when performance loses to politics, enthusiasm becomes a liability.

Why Good People Go Quiet Before They Quit

People rarely quit suddenly.

First, they withdraw emotionally.
Then, they disengage mentally.
Finally, they leave physically.

This silent exit begins the moment effort stops being rewarded.

They don't leave because work is hard.
They leave because hard work feels useless.

Organizations often misinterpret this silence as lack of ambition. But it is actually the sound of disappointment settling in.

And by the time leadership notices, it is usually too late.

Politics Rewards Short-Term Comfort, Not Long-Term Strength

Politics creates temporary stability.

Everyone agrees.
No one challenges.
Mistakes are hidden.

But organizations built on politics collapse slowly—from the inside.

Innovation dies because honesty dies first.
Growth stops because fear replaces feedback.
Talent leaves because meaning disappears.

Performance-driven cultures may feel uncomfortable—but they grow.
Politics-driven cultures feel comfortable—but decay.

A Gentle Truth for the Hardworking Reader

If you feel unseen today, it does not mean you are unworthy.

It means you are operating in a system that measures noise, not depth.

Your discipline still matters.
Your integrity still matters.
Your skills still matter.

Even if they are not applauded here.

Politics may win rooms—but performance wins time.

You may lose recognition today, but competence always outlives convenience.

Choosing Self-Respect Over Shortcuts

Not everyone is built for politics—and that is a strength.

You can learn visibility without losing values.
You can build influence without sacrificing honesty.
You can grow without becoming someone you dislike.

The goal is not to fight politics blindly—but to understand it without letting it change your core.

Because when performance loses to politics, the real test is not professional.

It is personal.

Will you let the system define your worth?
Or will you continue to grow—even quietly—until the right place recognizes you?

Politics may decide promotions.
But character decides peace.

And in the long run, peace is the promotion that matters most.

Chapter 4: Corporate Chanakya Was Right — Leaders Should Be Fair

When Leadership Forgets Its Duty

There is a quiet expectation every employee carries into the workplace.

Not promotion.
Not power.
Not privilege.

Just fairness.

We expect that effort will be seen, honesty will be respected, and mistakes—whoever makes them—will be addressed with the same standard. This expectation is not idealism. It is the foundation of trust.

But when leadership fails this basic duty, the damage goes far beyond targets and timelines. It enters the minds and hearts of people who once believed in the system.

As **Radhakrishna Pillai explains in *Corporate Chanakya***, true leadership is not about authority—it is about **dharma**, righteous conduct. And one of the strongest pillars of that dharma is impartiality.

Why Leaders Must Praise Performers Publicly

Chanakya believed that recognition is not just reward—it is direction.

When a leader praises a performer publicly, three things happen:

1. The performer feels seen.
2. The team understands what excellence looks like.
3. Trust in leadership deepens.

Public praise is not about ego. It is about clarity.

It tells the organization, *"This is the behavior we value."*

Yet in many workplaces, praise is selective. It is given based on comfort, closeness, or convenience—not contribution. The real performers are often thanked privately, while favorites are celebrated loudly.

This reversal quietly breaks morale.

When performance is not acknowledged openly, people stop stretching themselves. They do only what is safe. Over time, excellence becomes invisible, and mediocrity becomes normal.

Chanakya warned rulers against this exact mistake. A king who ignores merit, he said, weakens his own kingdom.

The same applies to modern organizations.

Why Favorites Must Be Corrected Openly When Wrong

Correcting a favorite privately may seem kind—but it is deeply unfair.

When others see a favored employee make mistakes without consequences, the message is loud:
Rules are flexible—for some.

Chanakya was firm on this: **those closest to power must be held to higher standards, not lower ones**. Why? Because favoritism is contagious. Once people believe fairness is optional, ethics collapse.

Correcting favorites openly is not humiliation. It is leadership integrity.

It tells the team:

- No one is above accountability
- Performance matters more than proximity
- Respect is earned, not gifted

When leaders avoid correcting favorites publicly, they protect comfort at the cost of credibility.

And once credibility is lost, authority becomes hollow.

How Bias Slowly Destroys Leadership Credibility

Bias does not destroy leadership overnight.

It starts subtly.

A skipped comment.
A delayed response.
An unexplained promotion.

Over time, patterns form. People notice who is heard—and who is ignored.

Soon, decisions are no longer questioned openly. Not because they are right—but because speaking up feels pointless. Silence becomes survival.

At this stage, leadership may still hold power—but it no longer holds respect.

Chanakya warned that a leader surrounded only by agreement is already in danger. When leaders prefer echoes over truth, they lose the ability to self-correct.

Bias does not just hurt employees.
It blinds leaders themselves.

Hard Truth: Not All Bosses Are Leaders

This is a difficult realization—and an important one.

A boss has authority.
A leader has responsibility.

A boss demands loyalty.
A leader earns trust.

Many bosses are promoted for technical skill or tenure, not leadership maturity. They may manage work well—but fail to manage people fairly.

This does not make them evil.
It makes them unprepared.

But the impact on employees is real.

Working under such leadership can make even the most sincere professional feel invisible, conflicted, and emotionally drained.

How to Work Ethically When Leadership Fails

This is where wisdom is required—not rebellion, not resignation.

When leadership fails, you have three choices:

- Become bitter
- Become political
- Become conscious

Chanakya never advised blind obedience. He advised **intelligent survival without moral collapse**.

Here is how to do that.

1. Separate Your Values from Their Behavior

Do not lower your standards just because leadership has lowered theirs.

Integrity is not situational. If you abandon it to fit in, you lose more than a promotion—you lose self-respect.

Work with excellence not to impress, but to honor your own discipline.

2. Learn Visibility Without Flattery

Being ethical does not mean being invisible.

Document your work.
Share outcomes, not complaints.
Speak facts, not emotions.

Visibility built on results is not politics—it is professionalism.

3. Observe Without Absorbing

Watch how bias operates—but don't let it infect you.

Understanding politics helps you navigate. Becoming political corrodes you.

There is a difference.

4. Build Strength Beyond One Leader

Chanakya believed dependence is weakness.

Upgrade your skills.
Expand your network.
Prepare for environments that value merit.

The strongest professionals do not wait for validation from broken systems.

They outgrow them.

The Quiet Power of Ethical Consistency

Ethical professionals often feel disadvantaged in biased systems. But over time, consistency builds a reputation that politics cannot erase.

Leaders change.
Organizations evolve.
But character compounds.

The favorite of today may struggle tomorrow.
The ignored performer may rise elsewhere.

Chanakya taught that time is the greatest judge.

A Final Reflection

Leadership is not tested when things are easy.

It is tested when:

- A favorite fails
- A performer succeeds
- Fairness is inconvenient

When leaders choose comfort over courage, organizations pay the price.

But when employees choose integrity over imitation, they protect something far more valuable than a title.

Their inner alignment.

And in the long journey of a career, that alignment becomes your greatest strength—even when leadership forgets its duty.

Chapter 5: Why Bosses Love Puppets

At some point in our professional lives, many of us face a confusing moment.

We work hard.
We stay honest.
We deliver results.

Yet someone else—less capable, less consistent, sometimes less sincere—moves ahead faster.

It hurts, not because we want shortcuts, but because we believed effort mattered.

This chapter is not written to make you angry.
It is written to help you understand.

Because once you understand *why* bosses love puppets, you stop blaming yourself—and you stop fighting the wrong battle.

Puppets Don't Challenge Authority

A puppet never asks uncomfortable questions.

They don't ask *why* something is done a certain way.
They don't suggest better alternatives that may expose inefficiencies.
They don't bring data that contradicts the boss's assumptions.

Not because they agree—but because they fear disagreement.

For an insecure boss, this feels like loyalty.

In reality, it is submission.

True professionals challenge ideas, not people. They speak for the work, the team, and the organization. But insecure leadership hears questions as threats.

So the puppet is rewarded—not for intelligence, but for silence.

Puppets Feed the Boss's Ego

Every insecure leader has an unspoken hunger: validation.

Puppets are experts at feeding it.

They praise decisions before results appear.
They agree even when logic disagrees.
They repeat the boss's words in meetings as if they were wisdom.

This constant admiration feels good. It soothes doubt. It creates an illusion of greatness.

But here is the truth no one says aloud:

Ego-fed leadership grows blind.

A boss surrounded by puppets slowly loses touch with reality. Decisions are no longer tested. Mistakes are hidden. Problems are sugar-coated.

And when reality finally hits—it hits hard.

Puppets Protect Insecurity

This is the hardest truth to accept—and the most important.

Favoritism is rarely about love.
It is about fear.

Fear of being outperformed.
Fear of being questioned.
Fear of being exposed.

A capable, independent employee can unintentionally trigger that fear. Not by arrogance—but by competence.

Your clarity makes their confusion visible.
Your confidence highlights their doubt.
Your growth threatens their control.

So instead of growing stronger, they build a comfort zone of obedience.

Puppets are safe.
Talent feels risky.

This Is Not About You Being Weak

Let this sentence settle in your heart:

Being overlooked does not mean you are weak.
It often means you are strong in the wrong environment.

Many talented professionals internalize rejection. They wonder if they should speak less, flatter more, or change who they are.

That is emotional self-harm.

Chanakya warned rulers against confusing loyalty with competence. A kingdom led by yes-men collapses quietly.

Similarly, an organization that promotes puppets stagnates while pretending to move forward.

The Silent Cost of Puppet Culture

When puppets rise, three things happen:

1. **Real talent disengages**
   People stop giving their best. They do only what is required. Passion fades.
2. **Innovation dies**
   No one wants to suggest improvements that may upset power.
3. **Insecurity multiplies**
   Puppets remain dependent. They cannot survive without protection.

The tragedy is that everyone loses—especially the boss.

Why Real Talent Doesn't Need Protection

Here is where the story shifts.

Talented professionals don't need safety umbrellas. They don't cling to one leader. They don't panic when management changes.

Why?

Because their strength is internal.

They carry skills, adaptability, and confidence that travel with them.

Puppets, on the other hand, live in constant anxiety:
What if the boss leaves?
What if priorities change?
What if someone finally notices the gap?

Insecurity becomes their shadow.

Stop Competing Emotionally

One of the biggest mistakes talented people make is emotional competition.

They compare praise.
They count promotions.
They replay unfair moments.

This drains energy and clarity.

You cannot win an emotional game in a biased system.

Instead, step out of it.

Detachment is not weakness—it is strategy.

Start Positioning Intelligently

Intelligent positioning is quiet. It is patient. It is powerful.

Here's how it works.

Build Value That Outlives Individuals

Skills that matter across teams, tools that scale, knowledge that solves real problems—these survive leadership changes.

Be Visible Without Being Political

Share outcomes, not opinions. Let results speak where words fail.

Create Options

When you are not desperate for one approval, you become mentally free.

Options are power.

Protect Your Self-Respect

Never trade dignity for validation. Promotions achieved through flattery cost more than they give.

A Gentle Truth

Not every workplace deserves your best years.

Some systems are designed to reward obedience, not excellence.

That does not make you wrong.

It simply means your future may belong elsewhere.

And when the day comes that leadership changes—as it often does—the puppets will search for safety, while talent will walk forward without fear.

Bosses love puppets because puppets make leadership feel easy.

But real growth is never easy.

If you feel unseen today, remember this:
You were not ignored because you lacked value.
You were ignored because someone else lacked courage.

And courage—unlike favoritism—can be learned, built, and carried anywhere.

Chapter 6: Why the Best Employees Quit

A Practical Survival Guide for the Quietly Strong

The best employees rarely quit loudly.

They don't slam doors.
They don't send angry emails.
They don't make dramatic exits.

They leave silently—after trying everything.

This chapter is not about weakness.
It is about fatigue.

Not physical tiredness, but **emotional exhaustion**—the kind that builds when effort goes unnoticed, integrity feels expensive, and staying honest starts to feel lonely.

They Quit When Growth Stops Feeling Fair

High performers don't expect special treatment.
They expect **fair treatment**.

They are willing to wait.
They are willing to improve.
They are willing to learn.

But when they repeatedly see:

- mediocre work rewarded,
- obedience promoted over originality,
- and visibility replacing value,

something inside them shifts.

Motivation does not die suddenly.
It erodes slowly.

They Quit When Feedback Turns One-Sided

Good employees crave feedback—not flattery.

They want to know:

- What can I do better?
- Where can I grow?
- How can I contribute more?

But in political environments, feedback becomes selective.

Favorites are protected.
Performers are pressured.

Mistakes by puppets are excused.
Mistakes by talent are magnified.

Over time, feedback stops feeling developmental and starts feeling punitive.

That is when silence begins.

They Quit When Psychological Safety Disappears

Psychological safety is not comfort.
It is **permission to be honest without fear**.

When speaking up leads to labeling, isolation, or punishment, smart people stop talking.

They attend meetings—but disengage mentally.
They deliver work—but stop investing emotionally.

And once emotional investment is gone, exit becomes inevitable.

They Quit When Their Values Feel Compromised

The best employees have strong inner compasses.

They struggle when asked to:

- take credit for others' work,
- stay silent about unethical behavior,
- support decisions they know are wrong.

Compromise once feels manageable.
Compromise repeatedly feels corrosive.

At some point, staying costs more than leaving.

The Silent Exit Begins Long Before Resignation

Here is a truth managers often miss:

People quit months before they resign.

They stop proposing ideas.
They stop volunteering.
They stop believing.

By the time the resignation email arrives, the emotional goodbye is already complete.

A Practical Survival Guide (Before You Decide to Quit)

Not every situation requires immediate exit.
Sometimes, clarity—not courage—is what's missing.

Before you resign, consider these survival steps.

1. Separate Identity from Workplace Validation

Your worth is not defined by one manager's opinion.

If your confidence rises and falls with recognition, politics will destroy your peace.

Build self-respect outside your job:

- skills,
- networks,
- learning,
- purpose.

Detachment restores power.

2. Document, Don't React

In political environments, memory becomes selective.

Keep records:

- achievements,
- feedback,
- contributions.

Not for revenge—but for clarity.

Documentation protects truth when narratives shift.

3. Stop Over-Explaining

Talented employees often over-explain to be understood.

In biased systems, over-explaining weakens perception.

Let results speak.
Let consistency speak.
Let calm speak.

Silence, when strategic, is strength.

4. Invest Where You're Valued, Not Tolerated

Observe carefully.

Who listens?
Who respects ideas?
Who supports growth?

Redirect your energy toward people who see value—not those who exploit effort.

5. Prepare Quietly

Preparation is not betrayal.

Update skills.
Strengthen networks.
Explore options.

You don't need to announce dissatisfaction to plan a better future.

Options create emotional safety.

When Leaving Becomes the Healthiest Choice

Sometimes, the bravest act is departure.

Not out of anger.
Not out of ego.
But out of self-respect.

Leaving a toxic system is not failure—it is alignment.

Great professionals do not cling to broken environments hoping they will change.

They choose growth over loyalty.

What Organizations Lose When the Best Quit

When the best employees leave, organizations lose:

- institutional knowledge,
- ethical anchors,
- innovation drivers,
- cultural balance.

What remains is comfort—not competence.

And comfort never builds great futures.

A Final Word to the Quietly Strong

If you are tired, it does not mean you are weak.

It means you have been strong for too long in a system that did not deserve it.

Whether you stay or leave, remember this:

Your integrity is an asset.
Your skill is transferable.
Your dignity is non-negotiable.

And the world—inside or outside that office—still needs people like you.

Chapter 7: The Silent Exit of Talent

Why Companies Lose Potential—and How You Protect Yours

Most people don't leave organizations because of work.

They leave because of **emotional erosion.**

This chapter is not about fighting office politics.
It is about outgrowing them—without losing yourself in the process.

Why the Best Employees Quit (Without Making Noise)

The best employees are rarely impulsive quitters.

They stay longer than they should.
They hope longer than they should.
They explain away red flags longer than they should.

They quit only after realizing one painful truth:

"Staying is costing me more than leaving."

They leave when:

- effort stops being acknowledged,
- growth stops being fair,
- and dignity starts feeling negotiable.

This is not entitlement.
This is emotional intelligence.

Quiet Quitting Is Not Laziness—It Is Self-Preservation

Quiet quitting is often misunderstood.

It is not about doing less work.
It is about withdrawing emotional labor.

People still deliver.
They still attend meetings.
They still meet deadlines.

But something invisible is gone:

- curiosity,
- ownership,
- innovation.

Quiet quitting is the body's way of saying,
"I will protect what this environment keeps taking."

Emotional Withdrawal Happens Before Physical Exit

Before resignation letters, there is silence.

- Ideas are no longer shared.
- Feedback is no longer sought.
- Risks are no longer taken.

When employees stop caring, it is not rebellion—it is grief.

They are mourning the version of the workplace they once believed in.

Loss of Innovation and Trust Is the Real Cost

Organizations often worry about attrition numbers.

They should worry about **potential loss**.

When politics dominate:

- creativity declines,
- trust erodes,
- collaboration becomes transactional.

People stop asking, “What’s best for the company?”
They start asking, “What’s safest for me?”

That is when organizations stagnate—not because of lack of talent, but lack of trust.

Human Cost: Companies Don’t Lose People—They Lose Potential

Every talented employee who disengages takes with them:

- ideas that were never voiced,
- solutions that were never tried,
- leadership that was never developed.

Potential is invisible on balance sheets—but devastating to lose.

And the tragedy is this:
Most of that loss is preventable.

The No-Politics Career Strategy

This strategy is not about playing games better.

It is about **choosing clarity over chaos**.

Step One: Decide When to Stay

Stay when:

- learning is still happening,
- your values are not compromised,
- and at least one leader sees your work clearly.

Stay if:

- politics exist, but don't define outcomes,
- feedback is honest—even if uncomfortable,
- and growth feels possible, even if slow.

Staying is wise when the environment is imperfect—but not toxic.

Step Two: Decide When to Prepare

Prepare when:

- promotions feel disconnected from performance,
- conversations feel unsafe,
- and emotional exhaustion becomes normal.

Preparation is not betrayal.
It is responsibility.

Preparation means:

- upgrading skills,
- strengthening professional networks,
- understanding your market value.

You don't prepare because you want to leave.
You prepare so you are not trapped.

Step Three: Decide When to Walk Away—with Dignity

Leave when:

- integrity feels expensive,
- silence feels compulsory,
- and self-respect feels threatened.

Walk away quietly.
Professionally.
Without bitterness.

Your exit should reflect who you are—not what the environment became.

Leaving with dignity protects your future far more than staying in resentment.

How to Build a Career Without Playing Politics

Here is the truth few talk about:

Politics win in the short term.
Competence wins in the long term.

Focus on:

- deep skills,
- consistent delivery,
- emotional maturity.

Avoid:

- gossip as currency,
- validation addiction,
- comparison traps.

Your reputation should be portable—strong anywhere, not dependent on one boss.

Staying Calm in a Political Environment

You don't control systems.
You control responses.

- Don't personalize dysfunction.
- Don't over-explain excellence.
- Don't absorb what isn't yours.

Calm is a competitive advantage.
So is restraint.

A Final Reflection

If you are struggling right now, remember:

You are not behind.
You are not weak.
You are not invisible.

You are simply in an environment that doesn't know how to value depth.

Whether you stay, prepare, or leave—choose the option that protects your **long-term self**, not just your current role.

Because careers are long.
And dignity should last longer.

How to Protect Your Potential in a World That Often Rewards Noise Over Value

Most professionals do not fail because they lack talent.
They fail because they **stay too long in systems that quietly drain them**.

This chapter exists for people who still believe in dignity, depth, and doing work the right way—but are tired of being punished for it.

It is not about blaming organizations.
It is about **protecting the human behind the role**.

Why the Best Employees Quit (A Global Truth)

Across countries, cultures, and industries, the pattern is the same.

The best employees quit not because:

- work is hard
- pressure is high
- expectations are demanding

They quit because **meaning disappears**.

They quit when:

- effort stops translating into growth
- honesty starts feeling risky
- silence feels safer than speaking

This happens in New York, London, Bangalore, Berlin, Tokyo—everywhere.

Talent is universal.
Politics is universal too.

Quiet Quitting: The Global Language of Emotional Exhaustion

Quiet quitting is not rebellion.
It is not laziness.
It is not entitlement.

It is **emotional self-defense**.

People still show up.
Still perform.
Still deliver.

But the heart pulls back.

Why?

Because giving emotionally in a system that does not reciprocate is unsustainable.

Quiet quitting is what happens when people realize:

"If I give more, I will lose myself."

Emotional Withdrawal: The Most Expensive Exit

Organizations track resignations.
They rarely track **emotional exits**.

Emotional withdrawal looks like:

- fewer ideas
- safer decisions
- zero risk-taking
- minimum visibility

Innovation dies quietly this way.

Not because people are incapable—but because **they no longer feel safe to care**.

Loss of Innovation and Trust

Trust is the foundation of high-performing cultures.

When favoritism rules:

- trust collapses
- collaboration becomes transactional
- people optimize for survival, not success

Companies don't lose productivity first.
They lose **belief**.

And belief is hard to rebuild once broken.

Human Cost: Companies Don't Lose People—They Lose Potential

Every time a talented employee disengages, the company loses:

- ideas that could have saved time or money
- leadership that could have inspired teams
- solutions that could have changed outcomes

Potential leaves long before people do.

And potential rarely returns.

This strategy is designed to work **globally**, regardless of:

- country
- hierarchy
- culture
- industry

Because human psychology is universal.

1. Knowing When to Stay (With Awareness)

Stay when:

- learning still outweighs frustration

- feedback is imperfect but honest
- values are stretched, not violated

Staying does not mean surrendering.
It means **extracting value while maintaining boundaries**.

2. Knowing When to Prepare (Without Panic)

Prepare when:

- promotions feel disconnected from contribution
- conversations feel politically filtered
- exhaustion becomes emotional, not physical

Preparation is calm, not reactive.

It looks like:

- skill deepening
- reputation building
- quiet networking
- self-investment

Preparation restores power.

3. Knowing When to Walk Away (With Dignity)

Leave when:

- integrity feels like a liability
- silence feels mandatory

- self-respect feels negotiable

Do not burn bridges.
Do not overshare pain.
Do not seek validation at exit.

Walk away with grace.

Your character is your final résumé.

How to Win Without Playing Politics

You don't beat politics by copying it.
You beat it by **becoming unreplaceable without becoming bitter**.

Focus on:

- mastery, not popularity
- clarity, not chaos
- consistency, not drama

Let your strength be portable.

Portable talent never fears change.

Staying Calm in Political Systems

Calm is not weakness.
It is control.

- Don’t internalize dysfunction
- Don’t personalize bias
- Don’t argue with insecurity

Observe. Adapt. Decide.

Peace is strategic.

A Quiet Reminder

If you feel tired, unheard, or unseen:

You are not broken.
You are not naive.
You are not alone.

You are simply standing at the intersection of **values and reality**.

Choose wisely.
Choose consciously.
Choose yourself.

Each chapter of this by Rakesh contains-

1. **Relatable reality** (story/emotion)
2. **Psychological truth** (why it happens)
3. **Human cost** (impact on people & companies)
4. **Practical strategy** (what to do)
5. **Quiet empowerment** (hope, not hype)

This makes the book Promoting Puppets as-

- readable across cultures
- valuable to employees and leaders
- suitable for corporate gifting, leadership reading, and HR discussions

Who This Book Is For (Market Fit)

- Corporate professionals (mid to senior level)
- High-performers feeling stuck or undervalued
- Ethical leaders trying to build better cultures
- HR and people-managers
- Anyone tired of politics but unwilling to become cynical

Why This Book of Will Stand Out

Because it:

- speaks truth without rage
- offers solutions without manipulation
- validates pain without glorifying victimhood

It doesn't teach people how to play dirty.

It teaches them how to **stay human and still win**.

Chapter 8: Winning Without Licking the Boss

Outgrowing the System Without Losing Yourself

How to Rise Without Bowing

Most people think survival in corporate life requires compromise.

Compromise of values.
Compromise of honesty.
Compromise of self-respect.

That belief is what keeps many talented people stuck—working hard, staying quiet, and slowly shrinking themselves to fit broken systems.

But here is the truth no one tells you early enough:

You don't escape toxic systems by fighting them.
You escape by **outgrowing** them.

This chapter is not about rebellion.
It is about **evolution**.

Upgrading Skills Strategically (Not Randomly)

Hard work alone is no longer enough.
Neither is blind upskilling.

Strategic growth begins with one honest question:

"If I were to leave tomorrow, what skill would make me valuable anywhere?"

Strategic skills have three qualities:

- they solve real problems,
- they are hard to replace,
- and they compound over time.

Instead of collecting certifications for validation, focus on **capability**.

Learn skills that:

- reduce cost,
- increase revenue,
- improve efficiency,
- or simplify complexity.

The more problems you can solve independently, the less dependent you become on approval.

Growth that frees you is always intentional.

Becoming Useful, Not Loud

In political environments, loudness is often mistaken for leadership.

But volume does not equal value.

The most powerful professionals are rarely the noisiest in the room.
They are the ones people quietly rely on.

Becoming useful means:

- anticipating problems before they escalate,
- delivering clarity where there is confusion,
- and creating solutions without demanding credit.

Usefulness builds trust organically.

And trust outlives hierarchy.

Building Leverage Without Flattery

Flattery is fragile leverage.

It works only as long as the ego it feeds remains in power.

Real leverage comes from **indispensability**.

You build leverage when:

- people depend on your judgment,
- your absence creates visible gaps,
- and your contribution is difficult to replicate.

Leverage grows silently.

It is earned through consistency, not proximity to power.

When you have leverage, you don't need to bow.
You negotiate from calm confidence.

Grabbing Opportunities Ethically

Opportunities rarely announce themselves clearly.

They appear as:

- extra responsibility,
- unsolved problems,
- moments of uncertainty.

Ethical growth means stepping forward without stepping on others.

It means:

- taking ownership without stealing credit,
- speaking up without humiliating,
- leading without dominating.

The strongest careers are built without burning bridges.

Integrity is not a limitation—it is a long-term strategy.

Why Growth Scares Political Systems

Here is a quiet truth:

Political systems fear independent thinkers.

People who grow beyond approval cannot be controlled easily.
People who don't seek validation cannot be manipulated.

That is why growth sometimes attracts resistance.

Not because you are wrong—but because you are becoming free.

Detaching Emotionally While Growing Professionally

One of the hardest lessons in corporate life is learning to **detach without disengaging**.

You can care about your work without tying your worth to outcomes.
You can give effort without giving your peace.

Detachment protects clarity.

When emotions are regulated:

- decisions improve,
- confidence stabilizes,
- and reactions reduce.

Calm is not passivity.
Calm is precision.

When the System Notices You Have Outgrown It

At some point, something shifts.

Your voice carries weight.
Your presence feels steady.
Your work speaks before you do.

That is when systems respond in one of two ways:

- they make space for you,
- or they resist you.

Both are signals.

If space opens—step into it.
If resistance grows—prepare to move.

Either way, you win.

Outgrowing Without Becoming Bitter

Bitterness is what happens when growth is delayed by resentment.

Do not let unfair systems harden you.

You are not here to prove them wrong.
You are here to build something better—for yourself.

Growth with grace is the highest form of success.

Key Message (Read This Slowly)

You don't need to bow.
You don't need to beg.
You don't need to perform loyalty.

You need to:

- build skill,
- create value,
- and expand perspective.

When you outgrow the system, it no longer defines you.

Success That Doesn't Cost You Your Self-Respect

There is a quiet struggle many professionals face but rarely speak about.

The pressure to impress.
The pressure to agree.
The pressure to become someone you are not—just to survive.

This chapter is for those who refuse to trade dignity for visibility.

Because deep inside, you already know this truth:

Success that requires you to shrink yourself is not success.
It is surrender.

The Silent Pressure to Please

Most people don't wake up one day deciding to flatter their boss.

It starts subtly.

A laugh you didn't feel.
A nod you didn't agree with.
A silence when you should have spoken.

Over time, these small compromises add up.

Not externally—but internally.

You start questioning yourself:

- "Am I being too honest?"
- "Am I too straightforward?"
- "Should I just go along?"

That is how authenticity slowly erodes—not by force, but by fear.

Why Boss-Pleasing Feels Safer Than Excellence

Pleasing authority feels safe because it reduces friction.

It avoids conflict.
It avoids risk.
It avoids discomfort.

But safety has a hidden cost.

When your growth depends on someone's mood, your confidence becomes fragile.
When approval replaces alignment, clarity disappears.

You may move up—but you never feel steady.

And success without inner stability is exhausting.

The Difference Between Respect and Submission

Respect is earned.
Submission is performed.

Many confuse the two.

True respect looks like:

- clear communication,
- consistent delivery,
- calm disagreement when necessary.

Submission looks like:

- constant agreement,
- emotional dependency,
- fear-driven compliance.

Bosses may enjoy submission—but organizations collapse because of it.

Progress needs courage, not echoes.

Winning by Becoming Unshakeable

The strongest professionals don't chase approval.
They cultivate **inner steadiness**.

They are not rude.
They are not rebellious.
They are **anchored**.

Anchored people:

- listen carefully,
- speak thoughtfully,
- and don't rush to please.

They don't argue unnecessarily.
They don't flatter unnecessarily.

They act from clarity, not anxiety.

And clarity is magnetic.

How Calm Confidence Changes Power Dynamics

When you stop seeking validation, something interesting happens.

Conversations change.
Meetings change.
Perceptions change.

Calm confidence sends a powerful signal:
"I respect you—but I don't disappear for you."

That balance is rare.
And rarity commands attention.

You don't need to dominate.
You don't need to impress.

You just need to **stand firm without aggression**.

Handling Disagreement Without Damage

Disagreement is inevitable.
How you handle it defines your maturity.

Winning without licking the boss means:

- disagreeing without ego,
- expressing concerns without accusation,
- and accepting decisions without resentment.

You don't need to win arguments.
You need to win **trust**.

Trust grows when people know:
"You will speak honestly—and still commit fully."

That combination is powerful.

When Your Work Speaks Louder Than You Do

There is a deep peace in letting your work do the talking.

Not because you want to stay invisible.
But because you trust **consistency over performance**.

Work that speaks:

- doesn't need exaggeration,
- doesn't rely on spotlight,
- doesn't beg for recognition.

It builds a reputation that travels ahead of you.

And reputations outlive bosses.

The Inner Cost of Living a Double Life

One of the most painful experiences in corporate life is living divided.

One version at work.
Another version at home.
A third version in your own head.

Pretending is tiring.

Winning without flattery means **integration**—being the same person everywhere.

You don't lose energy managing masks.
You don't lose sleep replaying conversations.
You don't lose yourself.

That peace is success too.

What Happens When You Stop Trying to Be Liked

This is uncomfortable at first.

Some people misunderstand you.
Some may feel threatened.
Some may distance themselves.

Let them.

Not everyone is meant to travel with you.

When you stop chasing being liked, you gain something better:
being respected by the right people.

And respect is what builds sustainable careers.

The Long Game Always Favors Integrity

Flattery works quickly.
Integrity works slowly.

But slow growth is strong growth.

Years later, when leadership changes, when teams reshuffle, when organizations evolve—those who stood on skill and character remain standing.

Those who depended on personalities struggle.

Winning without licking the boss is not about today's comfort.
It is about **tomorrow's freedom**.

A Gentle Truth to Carry With You

If you ever feel tempted to compromise yourself just to fit in, pause and ask:

"Will this version of me be proud five years from now?"

Careers are long.
Lives are longer.

Choose the version of success that lets you sleep peacefully at night.

Final Reflection

You don't need to impress the boss.
You don't need to feed egos.
You don't need to perform loyalty.

You need:

- clarity,
- consistency,
- and courage.

Winning without licking the boss is not louder.
It is **deeper**.

And depth always lasts longer than noise.

Chapter 9: **Value Over Visibility**

Why Quiet Contribution Outlasts Loud Presence

In today's corporate world, being seen often feels more important than being useful.

Meetings reward the loudest voice.
Emails praise the fastest reply.
Visibility is mistaken for value.

But behind the noise, something troubling happens.

Real work—the kind that builds systems, solves problems, and carries organizations forward—often goes unnoticed. And slowly, silently, professionals begin to question themselves.

"Am I doing enough?"
"Should I speak more?"
"Should I market myself louder?"

This chapter is about resisting that pressure—and choosing substance over spectacle.

The Age of Noise

Modern workplaces are crowded with activity but starved of depth.

People talk constantly.
Ideas are repeated in different words.
Presentations are polished—but outcomes are shallow.

Noise creates the illusion of progress.

But progress is quiet.

It happens when someone stays late fixing a process no one asked about.
When someone prevents a problem before it becomes visible.
When someone thinks deeply instead of reacting quickly.

These acts rarely trend.
But they sustain organizations.

Why Visibility Feels Safer Than Value

Visibility gives immediate feedback.
Value often takes time.

When you speak, people notice.
When you deliver quietly, people assume.

This creates a dangerous temptation:
to perform rather than to contribute.

Over time, professionals begin optimizing for attention instead of impact.
They chase meetings instead of mastery.
They measure worth by exposure.

And in doing so, they lose something precious—focus.

The Cost of Being Constantly Seen

Always being visible is exhausting.

You monitor your words.
You monitor your tone.
You manage impressions.

This constant self-awareness pulls energy away from real work.

Value-driven professionals conserve their energy.
They don't feel the need to comment on everything.
They don't compete for airtime.

They choose depth over display.

And depth compounds.

What Real Value Looks Like

Value is not flashy.
It is reliable.

It shows up as:

- decisions that hold under pressure,
- systems that work even when no one is watching,
- knowledge that others depend on.

Value is felt, not announced.

It creates trust.
And trust creates influence.

You don't need to remind people you matter.
Your work does it for you.

Why Loud People Fade Faster

Visibility without substance has a short shelf life.

At first, loud contributors shine.
They appear confident.
They dominate discussions.

But over time, patterns emerge.

Ideas don't translate into results.
Problems resurface.
Promises remain words.

When outcomes are missing, attention turns into scrutiny.

Value-driven professionals may be invisible early—but undeniable later.

The Quiet Confidence of Skilled People

People who invest in skill develop a different posture.

They don't rush to speak.
They wait for clarity.

They don't exaggerate contributions.
They let results accumulate.

This calm is often mistaken for passivity—but it is strength.

Quiet confidence does not need validation.
It is rooted in competence.

Choosing Value Is a Long-Term Decision

Choosing value over visibility is not a short-term strategy.

You may be overlooked.
You may be underestimated.
You may feel invisible.

But invisibility is temporary.
Incompetence is permanent.

Value builds a foundation that cannot be shaken by:

- leadership changes,
- organizational politics,
- shifting priorities.

Because value is transferable.

When Visibility Finally Comes

Here is the paradox.

When value becomes undeniable, visibility follows naturally.

People seek your input.
Your opinion carries weight.
Your absence is noticed.

You don't chase recognition.
Recognition finds you.

And when it does, it rests on something solid—not performance, but proof.

The Inner Peace of Choosing Substance

There is deep peace in knowing your worth is not situational.

You don't panic when meetings change.
You don't feel threatened by louder personalities.
You don't compete emotionally.

You focus on growth.
On learning.
On mastery.

This inner stability protects you from burnout.

For Those Who Feel Invisible Today

If you are doing real work and feeling unseen—pause.

Visibility is temporary.
Value is cumulative.

The world doesn't always reward the right things immediately.
But it eventually recognizes what endures.

Keep building.
Keep learning.
Keep contributing with integrity.

Your time will come—not because you demanded attention, but because you deserved it.

Final Reflection

Visibility shouts.
Value whispers.

But whispers travel far when the room grows quiet.

In the end, organizations don't remember who spoke the most.
They remember who solved the hardest problems.

Choose value.

It will outlast the noise.

.

The Fortress Within—Staying Calm, Motivated, and Mentally Strong

The most dangerous thing about a toxic office isn't that it might stall your career—it's that it might change your soul. When you see incompetent peers handed the keys to the kingdom, your brain triggers a "fairness alarm." If left unchecked, this alarm leads to chronic stress. To survive, you must move from being a victim of the environment to being a master of your internal state.

1. Emotional Discipline: The 5-Second Filter

In a political environment, your emotions are often used as weapons against you. If you get angry, you're "difficult." If you cry, you're "weak."

- **The Tool:** Practice the pause. When you witness a blatant act of favoritism, give yourself five seconds before speaking. Emotional discipline isn't about *not feeling*; it's about choosing which feelings get a seat at the table.

2. Detachment Without Disengagement

This is the "Secret Sauce" of the long-term survivor.

- **Disengagement** is when you stop caring about the work (Quiet Quitting).
- **Detachment** is when you care about the work, but you stop tying your self-worth to the *reaction* of a toxic boss.

The Mindset: Treat the office like a laboratory. You are the scientist performing excellence; if the "Puppet Master" doesn't appreciate the results, it is a data point about *their* incompetence, not a reflection of your value.

3. Calm as Power

In a room full of panicked sycophants and ego-driven managers, the person who remains calm is the person who actually holds the power. Calmness unnerves the manipulative because they cannot find a "hook" to pull you into their drama.

Practical Tools for the Fortress

- **Mental Boundaries:** Create a "Closing Ceremony." When you leave the office (or close your laptop), physically wash your hands or change your clothes. Symbolically leave the puppets at the door. Do not let people you don't even like occupy "rent-free" space in your head during dinner.
- **Energy Management (The Battery Check):** Politics is exhausting. Stop trying to win every argument. Save your "battery" for the tasks that build your resume and the people who actually support you. If a meeting is a political circus, go into "Power Save Mode"—observe, but don't over-invest.
- **Confidence Without Arrogance:** Real talent doesn't need to shout. Arrogance is a shield for the insecure; quiet confidence is the weapon of the competent. Know your worth so deeply that you don't need a "Puppet Master" to validate it with a title.

Key Line:

"Politics can control outcomes—your title, your salary, your office size—but it can never control your character. That belongs to you alone."

Chapter 10: Beyond Puppets — Redefining Success

When Growth Means Leaving the Stage

For a long time, success was explained to us in simple terms.

A higher title.
A bigger team.
A seat closer to power.

We were taught to chase promotions as proof of worth, to remain loyal even when respect was absent, and to stay longer than we should because leaving felt like failure.

But life inside corporate walls teaches a deeper truth—one no orientation program ever mentions.

Not every promotion is growth.
Not every boss deserves loyalty.
Not every workplace deserves your best years.

This chapter is not about rebellion.
It is about clarity.

The Moment You Start Asking Different Questions

There comes a quiet moment in every professional's life.

Not dramatic.
Not loud.

Just a question that refuses to leave:

"Is this still helping me become who I want to be?"

This is the moment when success begins to change its meaning.

You stop asking:

- "How do I impress?"
- "How do I survive?"

And start asking:

- "Am I growing?"
- "Am I respected?"
- "Am I becoming smaller to stay relevant?"

That shift is not weakness.
It is maturity.

When Promotions Become Golden Cages

Promotions are meant to expand you.

But in political environments, they often do the opposite.

They come with:

- louder expectations,
- silent compromises,
- emotional exhaustion disguised as leadership.

You are given authority—but not autonomy.
Responsibility—but not respect.

Some promotions are rewards.
Others are traps.

Real growth does not require you to shrink your values.

Loyalty Without Respect Is Self-Betrayal

Loyalty is powerful—when it is mutual.

But blind loyalty to a system that does not protect your dignity slowly erodes your self-worth.

Staying loyal to a boss who:

- rewards flattery over integrity,
- punishes honesty,
- protects incompetence,

does not make you noble.

It makes you invisible to yourself.

True professionalism includes knowing when loyalty has turned into emotional debt.

The Courage to Admit a Place Has Outgrown You—or You Have Outgrown It

Not every exit is an escape.
Some exits are evolution.

There is no shame in outgrowing a workplace.
There is no failure in choosing peace over politics.

You can give your best years only once.

Give them where they are valued—not merely consumed.

Redefining Success on Your Own Terms

Success is not applause.
It is alignment.

It is waking up without dread.
It is working without pretending.
It is knowing your growth is not dependent on someone else's insecurity.

Success looks like:

- clarity over chaos,

- skill over survival,
- dignity over dependence.

And sometimes, success is walking away—quietly, respectfully, powerfully.

Beyond Puppets: Becoming Unshakeable

Puppets need strings.
They fear silence.
They depend on approval.

You do not.

You carry your value with you.
You take your skills wherever you go.
You do not collapse when authority shifts.

That is real freedom.

Ending Truth

Sometimes success is not winning applause inside the room.

It is realizing the room was too small for you.

Final Promise to the Reader

You were never weak.
You were never "not good enough."
You were never invisible by accident.

You were just surrounded by noise.

And now—you can choose silence, clarity, and growth.

Conclusion: A Letter to the Ones Who Stayed Too Long

If you are closing this book with mixed emotions—relief, sadness, courage—you are not alone.

This book was never meant to make you angry.
It was meant to make you honest.

Corporate politics did not break you.
It revealed you.

It showed you:

- how strong you can be without applause,
- how calm you can remain without control,
- how capable you are beyond validation.

The world may reward noise today.
But it always needs value tomorrow.

Wherever you go next—
go as yourself, not as a version shaped by fear.

Your career is not a performance.
It is a journey.

Walk it with dignity.

Beyond Puppets — Redefining Success

Not every promotion is growth.
Not every boss deserves loyalty.
Not every workplace deserves your best years.

This book was never written to make you angry.
It was written to make you aware.

If you've ever worked hard and stayed silent…
If you've ever watched louder, less capable people rise faster…
If you've ever questioned your worth because honesty didn't win…

This book is for you.

Corporate politics doesn't fail people by accident.
It quietly teaches good people to doubt themselves.

But here is the truth no one told you:

You were never weak.
You were never invisible by mistake.
You were never "not enough."

You were simply surrounded by noise.

Real success is not applause inside a broken system.
Sometimes success is outgrowing the room.

Carry your skills.
Carry your dignity.
Carry your calm.

And walk forward without bitterness.

Because puppets need strings.
But real professionals carry value.

ABOUT THE AUTHOR

Rakesh Singh is a thoughtful and emotionally driven author who writes about the unseen struggles, silent sacrifices, and inner lives of modern human beings. His writing gives voice to feelings people often carry but rarely express—especially men navigating responsibility, love, work, and identity in a fast-changing world.

He is the author of the widely appreciated books ***Under the Table***, **AI VS Human** and ***Man After Marriage***, both of which explore the emotional realities of life beyond appearances—where strength is quiet, pain is unspoken, and love is often misunderstood.

Rakesh completed his schooling at **Kendriya Vidyalaya, IIT Kharagpur (West Bengal),India** and has a strong professional background in technology. He is a **Microsoft Certified AI Data Engineer**, **Microsoft Copilot Expert**, and **Python certified from IIT Madras**, with participation in multiple AI tool workshops conducted at **IIT Delhi**. His deep exposure to technology gives him a rare perspective—allowing him to write not just about machines, but about the humans living alongside them.

Despite working in advanced technology, writing has remained his passion since school days. He has won multiple writing competitions within and outside the organizations he has worked with. His stories are shaped by real experiences, real emotions, and real people.

Through his books, Rakesh highlights the emotional cost of modern life—how men silently balance family, marriage, work, and expectations, and how technology, progress, and pressure often ignore human limits. He believes that while technology can replace skills, it can never replace **emotions, empathy, or the human soul**.

Currently based in **Gurugram, Haryana**, Rakesh continues to write with one purpose:
to remind the world that behind every role, responsibility, and achievement, there is a human being who deserves understanding.

www.ingramcontent.com/pod-product-compliance
Ingram Content Group UK Ltd.
Pitfield, Milton Keynes, MK11 3LW, UK
UKHW041315190726
13845UKWH00025B/272

9 789356 920835